Editorial Project Manager
Mara Ellen Guckian

Contributing Editor
Kelly McMahon

Managing Editors
Karen J. Goldfluss, M.S. Ed.
Ina Massler Levin, M.A.

Cover Artist
Marilyn Goldberg

Art Production Manager
Kevin Barnes

Art Coordinator
Renée Christine Yates

Imaging
James Edward Grace
Ricardo Martinez

Publisher
Mary D. Smith, M.S. Ed.

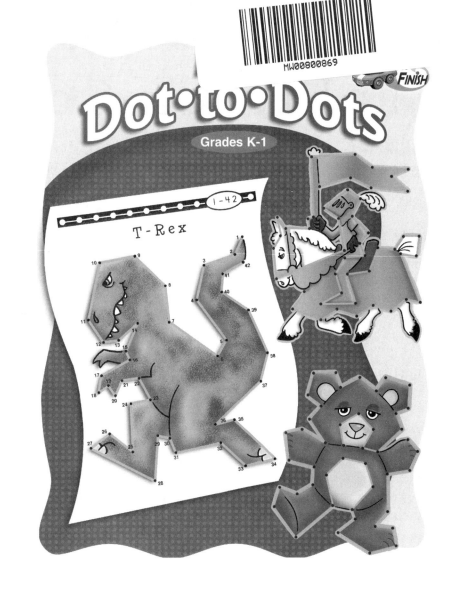

Illustrator

Kelly McMahon

Teacher Created Resources, Inc.
6421 Industry Way
Westminster, CA 92683
www.teachercreated.com

ISBN: 978-1-4206-5989-4

©2006 Teacher Created Resources, Inc.
Reprinted, 2008
Made in U.S.A.

Table of Contents

Introduction

Dot-to-dots are fun to do. They are also excellent activities to develop a number of early literacy skills including the following:

❑ *number recognition*—discerning which symbol stands for which numeral

❑ *sequencing*—knowing which number follows the next

❑ *fine motor skill development* (shoulder to wrist to hand)—holding the writing or coloring implements in the proper manner

❑ *eye–hand coordination*—guiding the writing tool in the desired direction

❑ *beginning drawing skills*

❑ *guessing and estimating skills*

The dot-to-dots pictures in this book progress from easy to challenging. Don't worry if some of the activities stump 5–7 year olds at first. Encourage them to work through these puzzles on their own, developing their planning and estimating skills. Allow children to help each other as they discover the answers to the more difficult pages.

The oval at the top of each page indicates the range of dots to be connected to complete the picture. An answer key is provided at the end of the book.

Recognizing numbers and connecting the dots in the appropriate sequence to finish a picture can be exciting. The completed pictures include a wide variety of subjects of interest to young children. Many children enjoy coloring the completed pictures.

Have fun!

Home Sweet Home

4

Under the Sea

High Flyer

6

Toothbrush

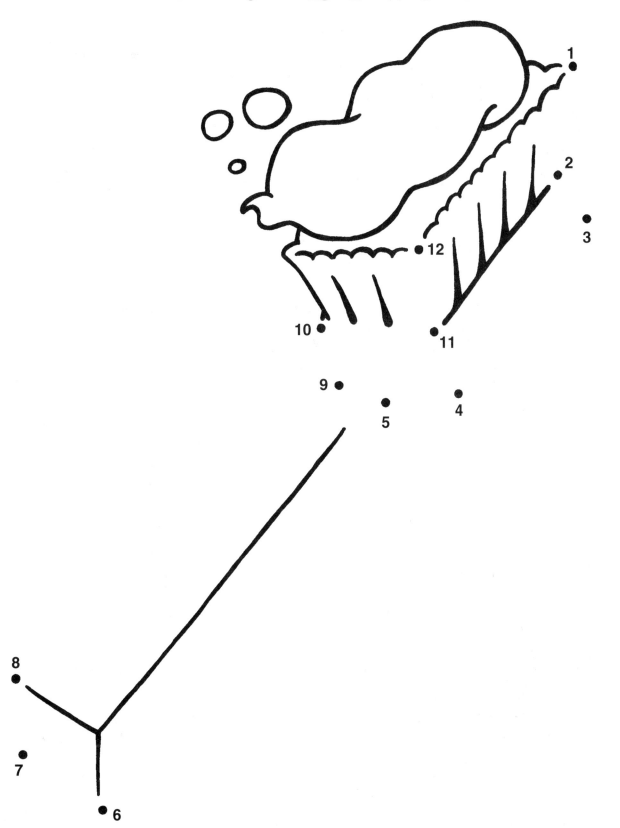

Mushroom

• 7

• 6

• 8

• 9

11 • — 3 •

• 5

10 • 4 •

• 2

12 •

13 • — • 1

Butterfly

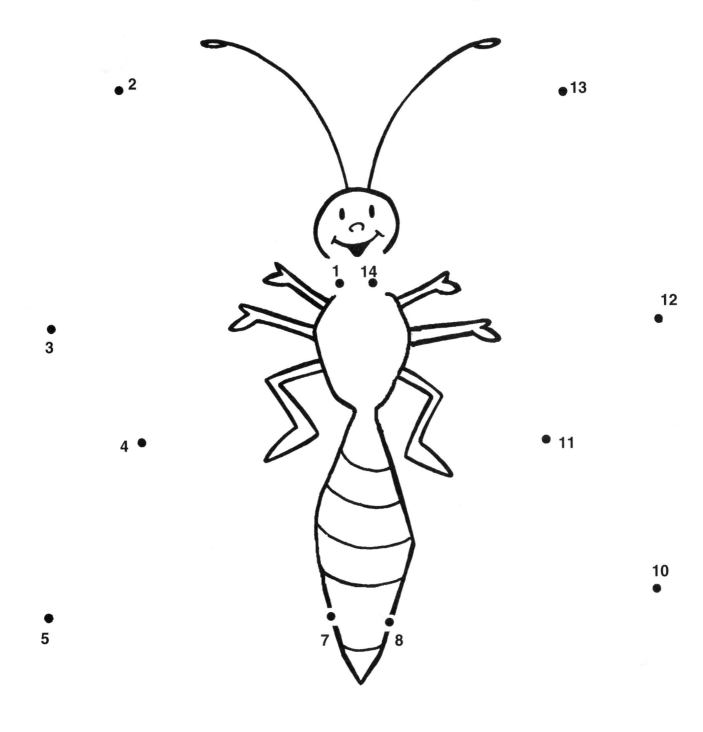

1-14

Home Run

Flying High

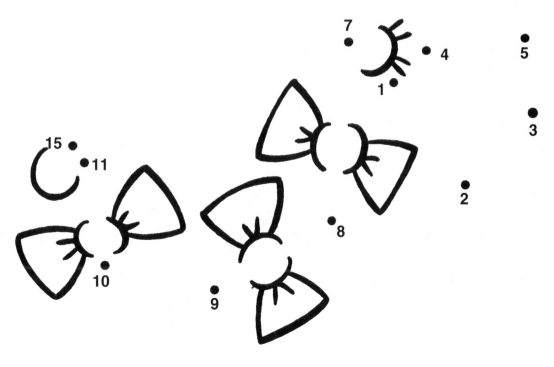

Float Down

Caterpillar

Candlelight

Swan

Bird in a Cage

Time to Nest

#5989 More Dot • to • Dots

Happy Birthday

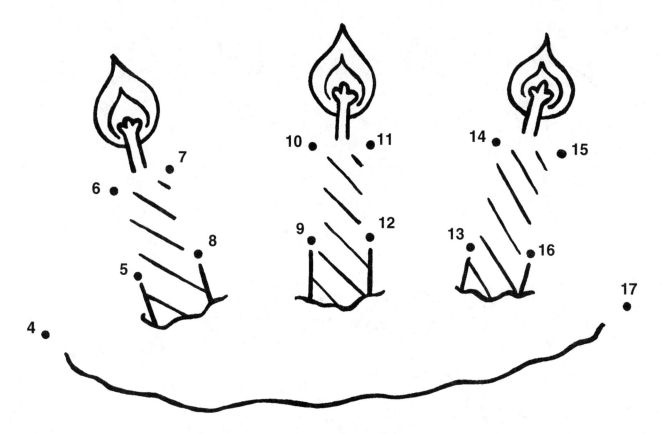

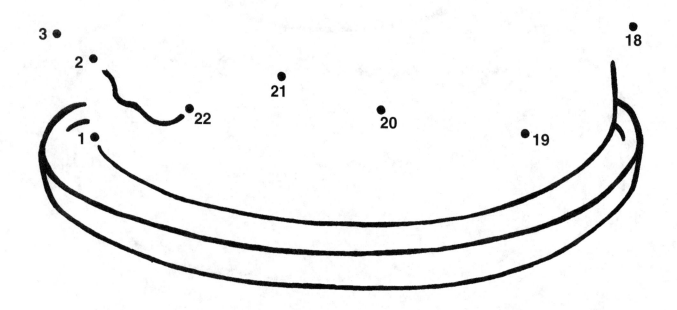

Lock and Key

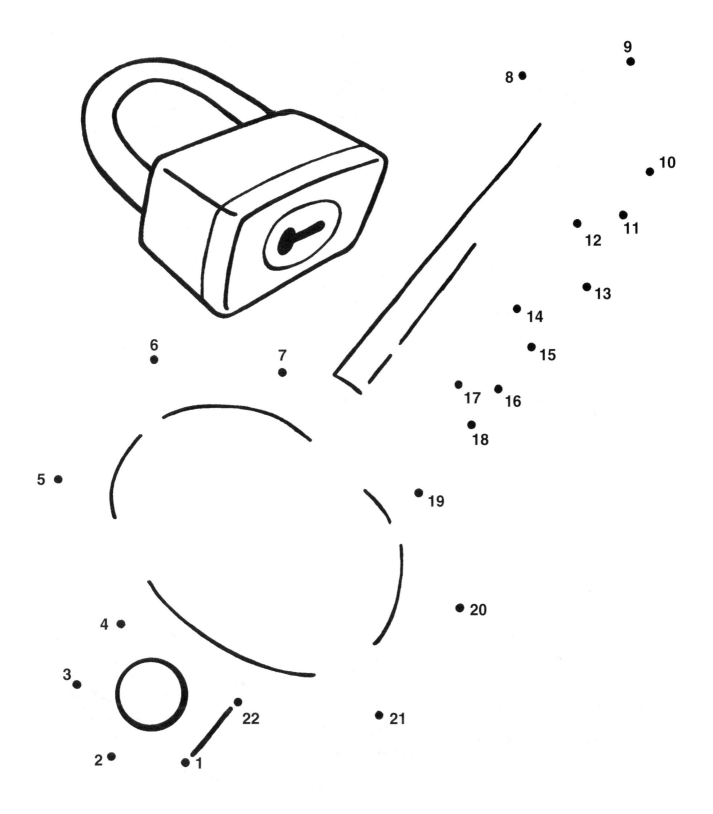

Hot Air Balloon

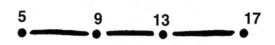

5   9   13   17

4

6

8   10

12   14

18

16

3

19

7   11   15   20

23

2   1

22   21

All Dressed Up

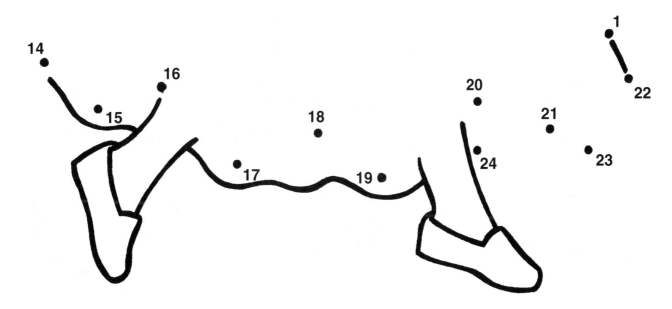

Ice Cream Cone

6 •   • 7

5 •

                                                      •8

                                                  • 9
4 •

3 •   •10

                                                              •11
                                                        •12
2 •   1 •   22 •   16 •
               21 •   •18
         •23   •25
                                                   •17
      20 •
            •19

                                                   15 •
                                                         •13
                                                      •14

                                    •24

Evergreen

●13

12● ●11 ● ●14
      ● 15●

10● ●9

17● ●16

7● 5● ●21 ●19
8●   ●18
6●
3●   20●
                23● 25●
1● 2● 4● 22● 24●

Rabbit

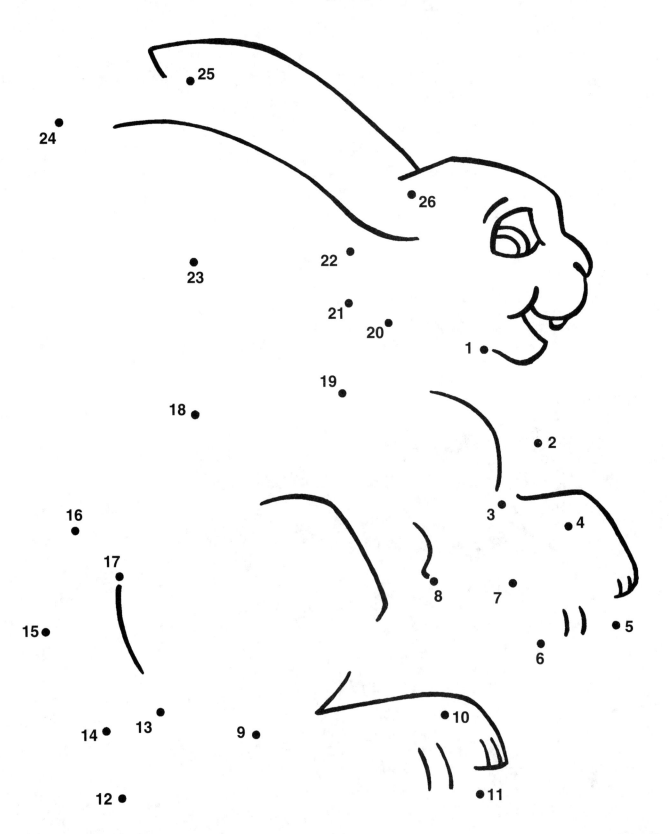

Ponytail

Flag

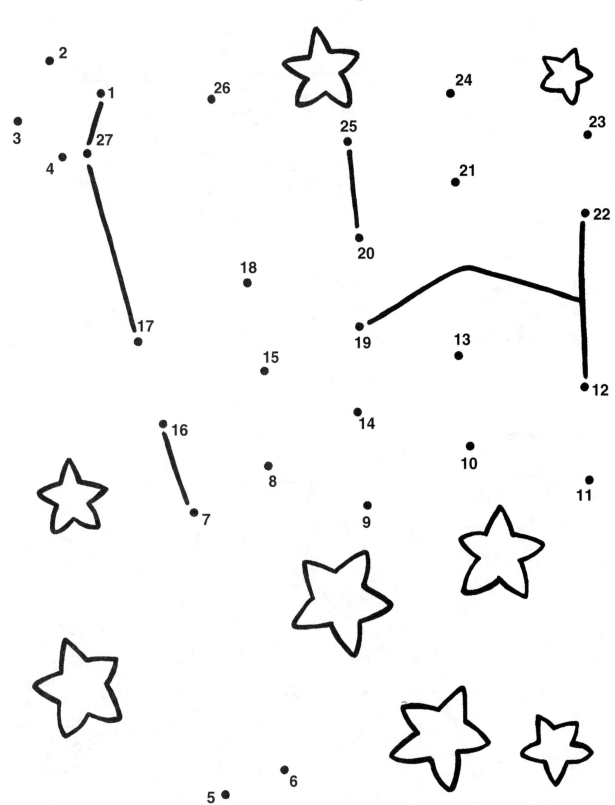

26

Shark

Mailbox

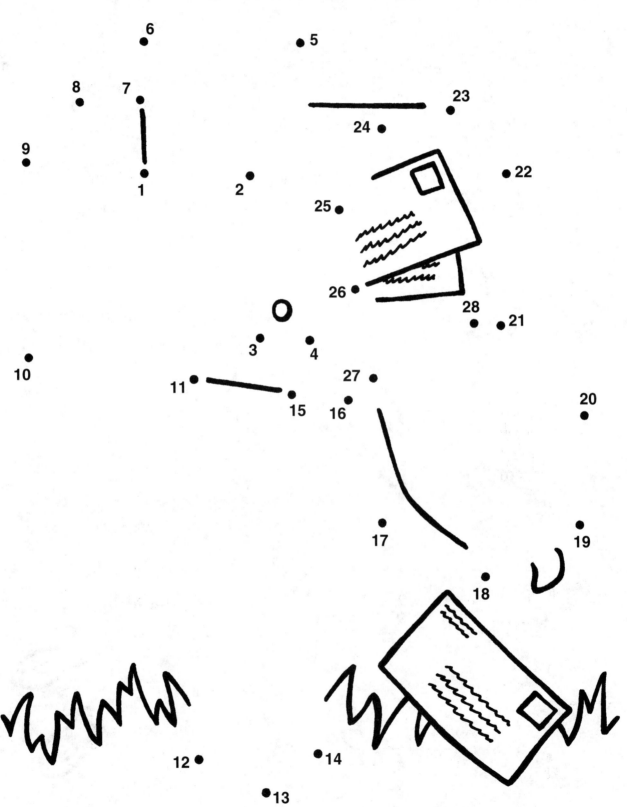

Mountain Home

Snowman

Pitcher of Milk

Time to Fish

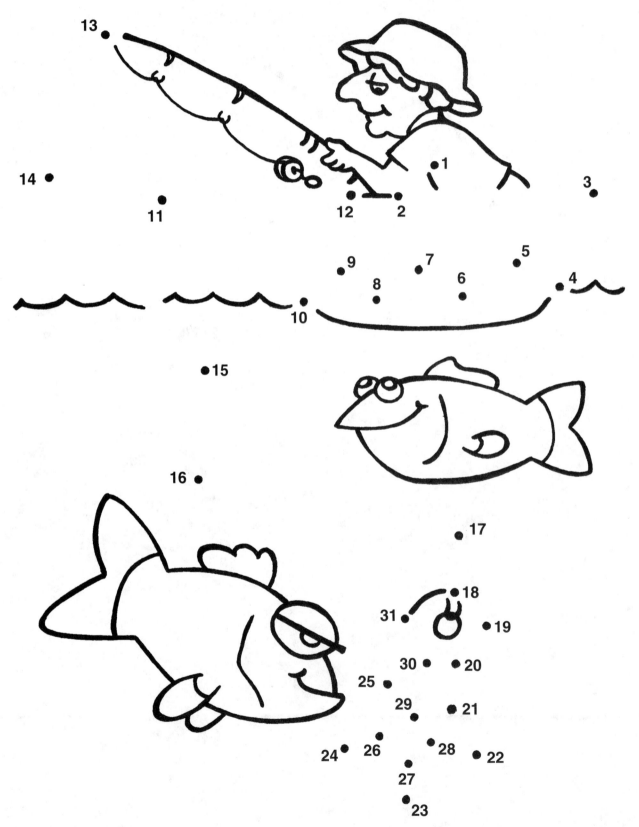

Tea Time

Off to Work

All Aboard

Scarecrow

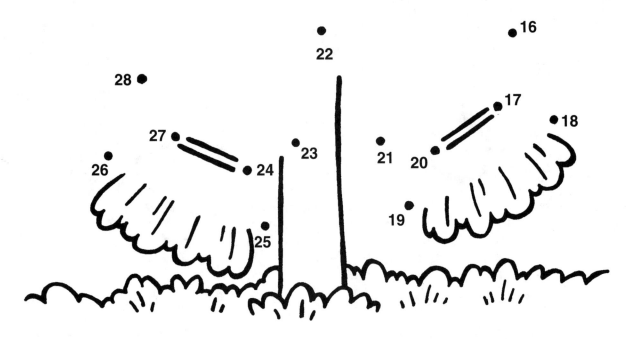

Helicopter

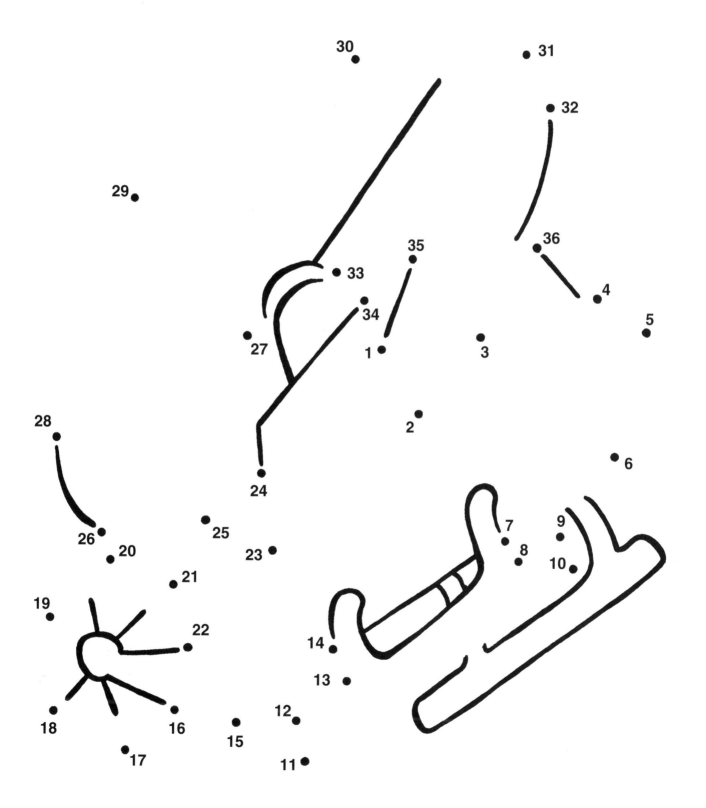

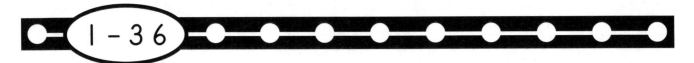

Poodle

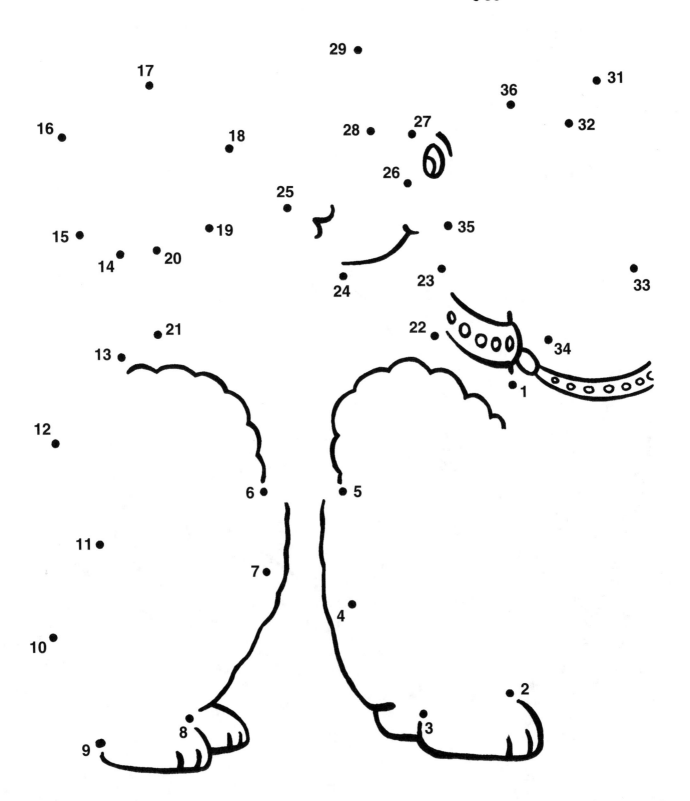

Umbrella

Rocking Horse

Treasure!

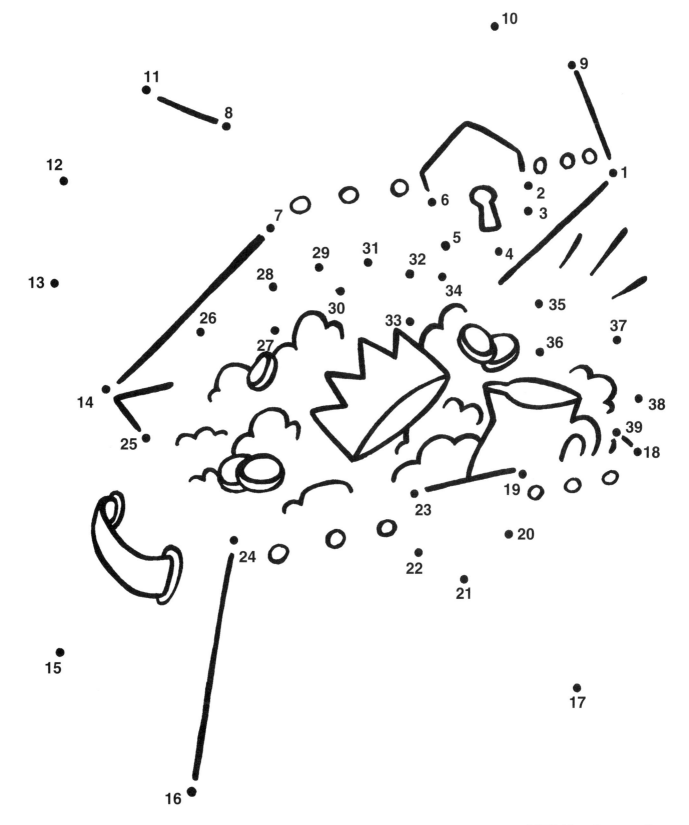

Giraffe

Deer

Chef

T-Rex

Cow

Whale

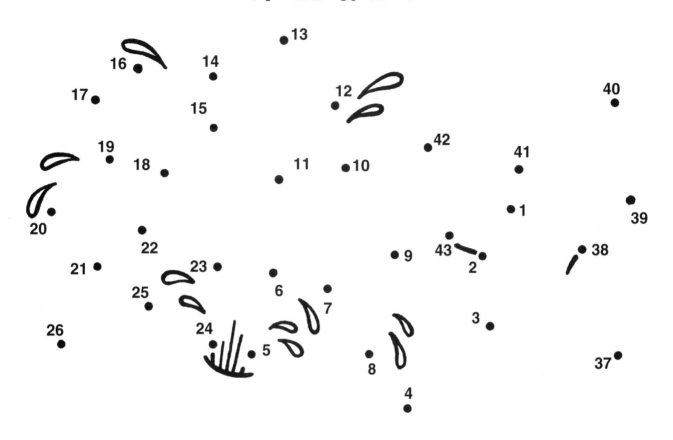

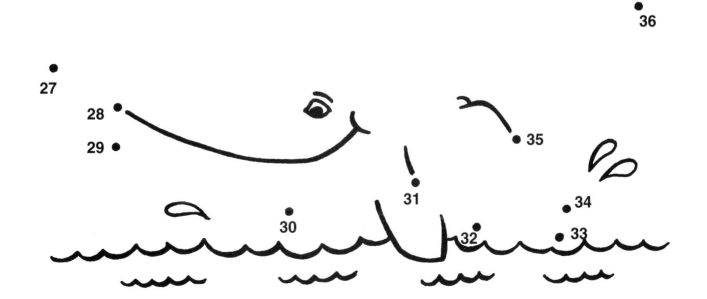

Summer Fun

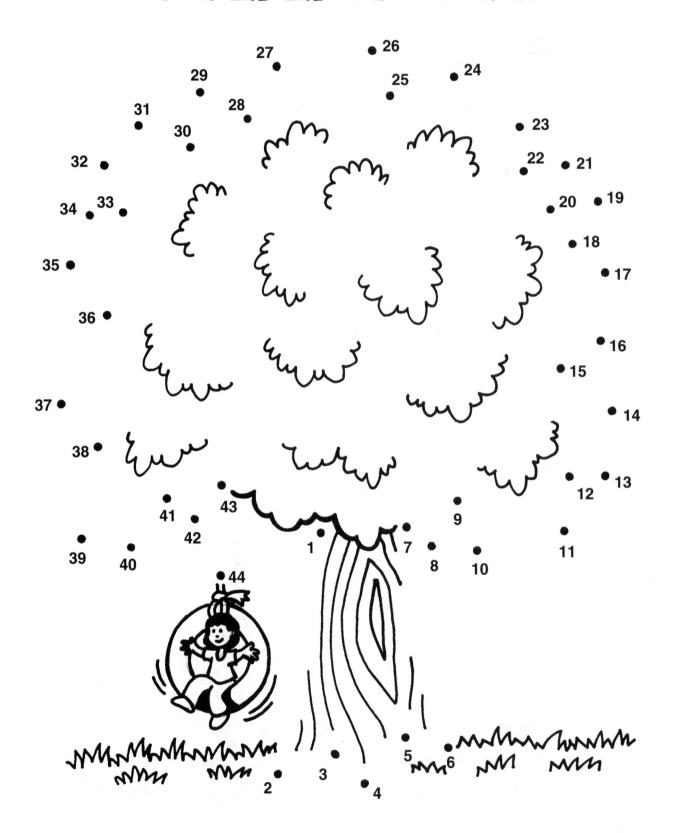

Back Hoe

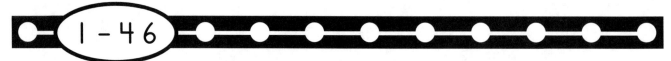

Teddy Bear

Car

Clown

Knight

Octopus

2

1

4

3

46

47

5

6

44

45

8

7

48

43

9

42

10

41

11

37   36

35   27

38   21

28   20   16

40   13

26   22   12

32   39   17

19   15

33   34   14

29   23

31   25   18

30   24

Lion

Monkey

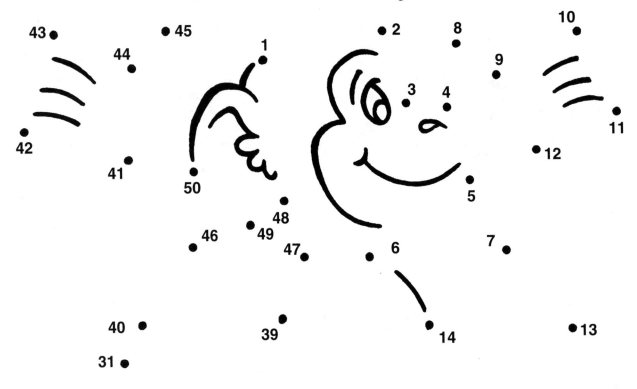

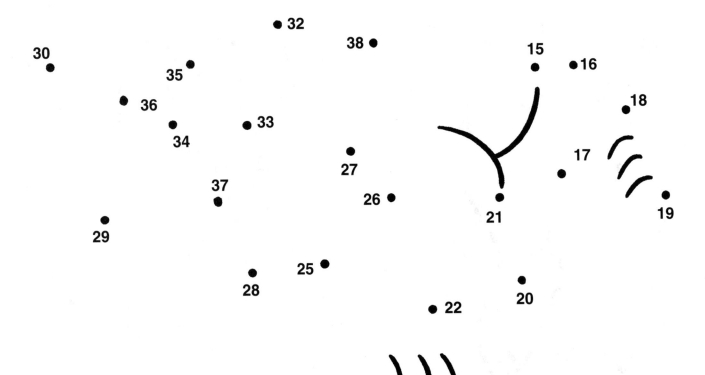

P o n y

Answer Key

Page 4

Home Sweet Home

Page 5

Under the Sea

Page 6

High Flyer

Page 7

Toothbrush

Page 8
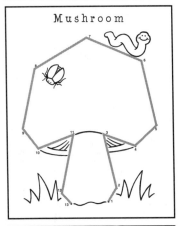
Mushroom

Page 9
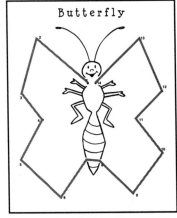
Butterfly

Page 10

Home Run

Page 11
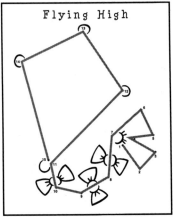
Flying High

Answer Key (cont.)

Page 12

Float Down

Page 13

Caterpillar

Page 14

Candle Light

Page 15

Swan

Page 16

Bird in a Cage

Page 17

Time to Nest

Page 18

Happy Birthday

Page 19

Lock and Key

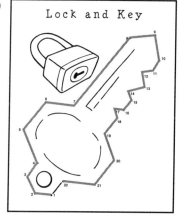

Answer Key *(cont.)*

Page 20

Hot Air Balloon

Page 21

All Dressed Up

Page 22

Ice Cream Cone

Page 23

Evergreen

Page 24

Rabbit

Page 25

Ponytail

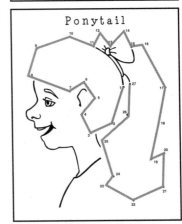

Page 26

Flag

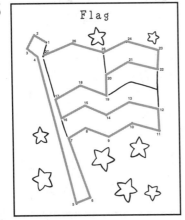

Page 27

Shark

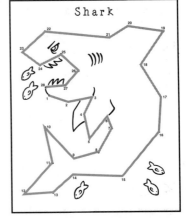

Answer Key *(cont.)*

Page 28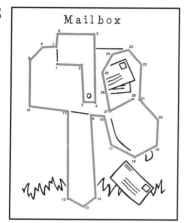

Page 29

Page 30

Page 31

Page 32

Page 33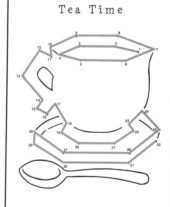

Page 34

Page 35

Answer Key *(cont.)*

Page 36

Scarecrow

Page 37

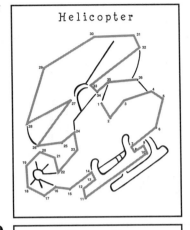

Helicopter

Page 38

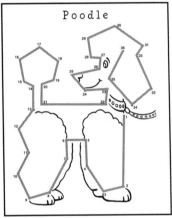

Poodle

Page 39

Umbrella

Page 40

Rocking Horse

Page 41

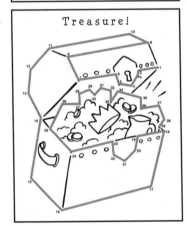

Treasure!

Page 42

Giraffe

Page 43

Deer

Answer Key *(cont.)*

Page 44

Chef

Page 45
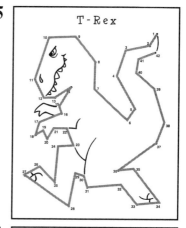
T-Rex

Page 46

Cow

Page 47
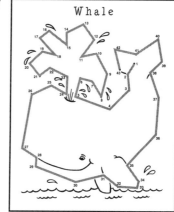
Whale

Page 48

Summer Fun

Page 49

Back Hoe

Page 50

Teddy Bear

Page 51

Car

Answer Key *(cont.)*

Page 52

Clown

Page 53

Knight

Page 54

Octopus

Page 55

Lion

Page 56

Monkey

Page 57

Pony